This Journal Belongs to:

_____

_____

About

The theory behind Manifestation & the use of the Law of Attraction

To manifest is "to show plainly; make visible or apparent."

When manifesting, you are calling something forth into your life that is not yet physically present. It is the manifestation of our thoughts, feelings, and desires. All of us have the ability to manifest our dreams into reality.

The first step is to get clear about what you want to manifest. This can be done through journaling, meditation and visualization.

Once you are clear about what it is that you desire, you can then take inspired action to turn your dreams into reality. There are many ways to manifest, some people use vision boards, others use affirmations or recite mantras. The most important part of manifesting is believing that what you desire is on its way.

One way to manifest on a daily basis is to keep a manifestation journal. You can use the opportunity to work through the different steps and record your progress along the way.

Manifesting our deepest desires is not magic - it's simply a matter of learning how to work with the laws of the universe.

There are many different ways to manifest our desires, but the magic ingredient is taking inspired action towards our goals. Whatever method we choose, the key is to be consistent in our practice. The more we focus on manifesting our desires, the more likely we are to see results.

So, if you're ready to start manifesting your dream life, let's start here today with this journal.

Create a daily practice by setting aside a few moments just for you, that you can dedicate towards focusing on your dreams and goals and planning the inspired action that will get you there.

This should be an exercise that is easy, one that you look forward to each day. Find a quiet and comfortable place where you can spend some time in quiet reflection.

How to

How to use this journal

 Exercise 1

Gratitude audit: Taking time to give thanks for where we are and what we have forms an excellent foundation for attracting more good into our lives. When we start to look around and recognize what we have to be grateful for we can't help but raise our vibration.

 Exercise 2

A day in the life of my future self: Have fun with this exercise, let your imagination run wild as you create a vision of what it will look like when all of your hopes and dreams come to fruition. Connect to the feelings and emotions of that which you desire.

 Exercise 3

What do I want to manifest? Use this exercise to get clear and specific about the things you want to manifest. Spending time here to give detail to what you want and why will make it easier to take the inspired action required.

 Exercise 4

What is currently holding me back? It's easy to stand in our own way and hold ourselves back from our true potential. Identifying ways in which we do this and uncovering repeated patterns is a great way to highlight alternative paths we can take to achieve different results.

 Exercise 5

Popular manifestation methods: What works best will be different for every person, so don't be afraid to experiment while finding the most effective ways for you. Manifestation should be fun and easy. When approached in the correct way, it will soon become effortless.

 Exercise 6

Ways to raise your vibration: Learning to raise your vibration is a powerful tool that can serve you when it comes to manifesting and beyond. By becoming a vibrational match to our dreams and goals, we can call them into our life with greater ease.

Steps of Manifestation

1 Gratitude

Gratitude is a powerful emotion that can have a profound effect on our lives. Gratitude has been shown to boost our moods, increase our resilience in the face of stress, and even improve physical health.

2 Visualize

By visualizing what you want to achieve or create, you can raise your vibration and attract more of what you desire into your life.

When you visualize, you are effectively calling in your desires and planting the seeds of your manifestation. The more you visualize, the more you will begin to see results.

3 Vibration

Raising your vibration is an essential step in the process of manifesting your desires using the law of attraction. This involves shifting your energy and focusing your mind on positive thoughts and feelings.

4 Eliminate

Many people struggle with removing old beliefs and habits that are no longer serving them. These blocks can get in the way of achieving our goals, making it hard to move forward and be successful. Thankfully, there are several effective techniques that can help us eliminate these blocks, including meditation, positive affirmations, and journaling.

5 Affirmations

When you repeat something to yourself often enough, eventually you start to believe it. This is why affirmations can be so powerful. By repetition, we can actually change our subconscious beliefs about ourselves.

6 Doubt and Fear

Let go of any doubts or fear that you cannot have what you desire.

7 Receive

Ask and you shall receive. Simple but powerful. Be open to receiving your manifestations when they show up.

8 Dream

It is time to start dreaming big. You are your only limit.

Exercise 1

Gratitude Audit

Let's get started by taking a look at where you are right now. One of the key steps to manifesting greater happiness is to start with the things that you already have. Take a moment to think of all of the great things you are grateful for right now. Gratitude is a great way to raise your vibration and open yourself to receiving more.

I am grateful for...

1

2

3

4

Exercise 2

A Day in the life of my future self...

The word 'manifestation' means to create something or turn something from
an idea into a reality. So let's start with that dream that you want to turn into reality!
Imagine for a moment that you have already manifested all that you desire - what
does life look like? Be as detailed and specific as you can to really explore what
you want and where you are headed.

Exercise 3

What do I want to manifest?

Manifesting starts with two key steps. Step one is clarity. Get specific about what you want - these can be small achievements or bigger goals. Step two is inspired action. What actions can you take today to move you closer to your goals and dreams?

My Goals

1

2

3

4

Actions to achieve these goals

⭕ **Goal #1:**

_____

_____

_____

_____

_____

⭕ **Goal #2:**

_____

_____

_____

_____

_____

⭕ **Goal #3:**

_____

_____

_____

_____

_____

⭕ **Goal #4:**

_____

_____

_____

_____

_____

Exercise 4

What's currently holding me back?

Before we can truly manifest the things we desire, it can be useful to spend time identifying areas where we feel stuck and where we can see things holding us back. Take some time to objectively review all areas of your life. Without adding judgement write down areas that don't align with your vision. As you put things on the page, visualize letting these things go and removing their power.

Blocks and Limitations

 1

 2

Blocks and Limitations

3

4

5

6

Exercise 5

Manifestation techniques & ideas

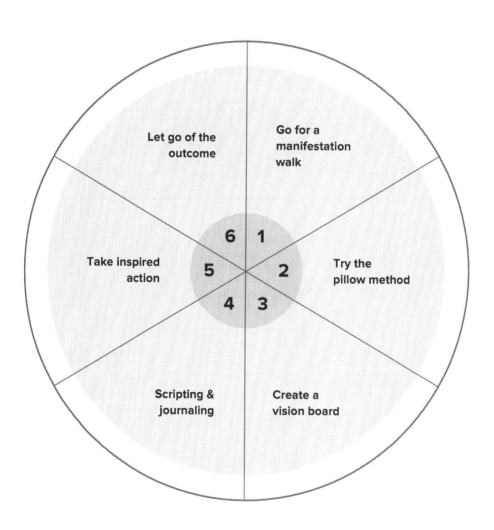

Let go of the outcome

Go for a manifestation walk

Take inspired action

Try the pillow method

Scripting & journaling

Create a vision board

6 1
5 2
4 3

Exercise 5

Manifestation techniques & ideas

1 **Go for a manifestation walk**

A manifestation walk is a guided visualization process that can help you connect with desired outcomes and create a roadmap for achieving them. While out walking, as you take each step imagine yourself taking steps towards your goal, picturing each action and outcome along the way.

2 **Try the pillow method**

This simple strategy involves writing down your goals on a piece of paper and placing it underneath your pillow before going to bed. Doing this allows you to tap into the power of your subconscious mind while you sleep, which is much more influential than your conscious mind.

3 **Create a vision board**

Vision boards help you visualize the life that you want, serving as a constant reminder of your priorities and aspirations. Whether you use pictures from magazines or paint your own creations, putting your heart and soul into creating a vision board helps solidify your intentions and gives them tangible form.

4 **Scripting & Journaling**

Scripting and journaling are powerful tools that can be used to enhance our mental well-being. Both practices differ in important ways. Scripting involves creating a detailed plan for our goals & dreams while journaling focuses more on free-flowing reflection and self-discovery.

5 **Take inspired action**

Once you know what you want, it's time to take inspired action towards making your dreams a reality. This could mean anything from signing up for a class or seminar related to your desired career, applying for a new job, or taking steps to improve your health.

6 **Let go of the outcome**

By dropping your attachment to a desired outcome, you can release any worry or doubt and move forward with complete confidence. Through the process of letting go and allowing the universe to work its magic, you can truly begin to manifest all that you wish for in life.

Exercise 6

How can I raise my vibration?

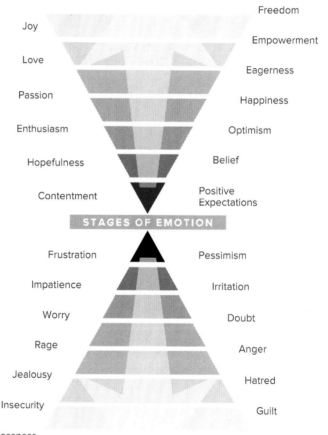

UPWARD SPIRAL

Freedom

Joy

Empowerment

Love

Eagerness

Passion

Happiness

Enthusiasm

Optimism

Hopefulness

Belief

Contentment

Positive Expectations

STAGES OF EMOTION

Frustration

Pessimism

Impatience

Irritation

Worry

Doubt

Rage

Anger

Jealousy

Hatred

Insecurity

Guilt

Powerlessness

DOWNWARD SPIRAL

What small things can I do in a given moment to raise my vibration and keep it high?

1

2

3

4

5

6

Affirmations

For A New Week

- Today I feel strong, confident, and empowered.
- My energy rises each day with the sun.
- My day is filled with joy and excitement.
- Today is a gift, and I embrace it with gratitude.
- I am happy & grateful for a fresh start and a brand new week.
- I am open to receive all of the miracles, magic & success coming my way.
- I bravely explore the possibilities behind every door of opportunity.
- I am equipped to handle anything that comes my way today with ease.
- I have all the tools & resources I need to succeed.
- I follow my intuition with courage, there is no obstacle I can't overcome.
- I am confident, brave, and prosperous.
- I generate pure love, light, and positivity to those around me.
- I am a powerful being and I am here to do good for this world.
- I move through this day shining my light wherever I go.
- I can choose faith over doubt and courage over fear.
- I welcome positivity in all areas of my life.
- I love and accept myself more & more each day.
- I feel good about the life I'm creating for myself, I am right where I should be.
- This week, I will live a happy, healthy, fulfilling life.
- I relish the fresh start and new beginning that Monday brings.
- This week is filled with limitless potential, I can achieve all I need.
- I have everything I need within me to create a happy life.
- I release all fear, doubt & uncertainty.

Manifestation
Journal

Daily Planner

Date: _____

1 Today I am manifesting:

_____
_____
_____

2 My intentions for today are:

_____
_____
_____

3 Today I am letting go of:

_____
_____
_____

4 Today I am grateful for:

_____
_____
_____

My daily affirmations:

Some of my thoughts

Daily Planner

Date: _____

1 Today I am manifesting:

----

2 My intentions for today are:

----

3 Today I am letting go of:

----

4 Today I am grateful for:

My daily affirmations:

Some of my thoughts

Daily Planner

Date: _____

1 Today I am manifesting:

_____
_____
_____

2 My intentions for today are:

_____
_____
_____

3 Today I am letting go of:

_____
_____
_____

4 Today I am grateful for:

_____
_____

My daily affirmations:

Some of my thoughts

Daily Planner

Date: _____

① Today I am manifesting:

----

② My intentions for today are:

----

③ Today I am letting go of:

----

④ Today I am grateful for:

My daily affirmations:

Some of my thoughts

Daily Planner

Date: _____

1 Today I am manifesting:

_____

_____

_____

2 My intentions for today are:

_____

_____

_____

3 Today I am letting go of:

_____

_____

_____

4 Today I am grateful for:

_____

_____

Some of my thoughts

Daily Planner

Date: _____

My daily affirmations:

1 Today I am manifesting:

_____

_____

_____

2 My intentions for today are:

_____

_____

_____

3 Today I am letting go of:

_____

_____

_____

4 Today I am grateful for:

_____

_____

Some of my thoughts

Daily Planner

Date: _____

1 Today I am manifesting:

_____

_____

_____

2 My intentions for today are:

_____

_____

_____

3 Today I am letting go of:

_____

_____

_____

4 Today I am grateful for:

_____

_____

_____

My daily affirmations:

Some of my thoughts

Weekly Reflection

What was my top accomplishment this week?

What showed up that I wasn't expecting?

What made me happy this week?

What obstacles did I overcome this week?

What clues have I noticed that I am starting to manifest my dreams?

1
2
3
4

Final thoughts

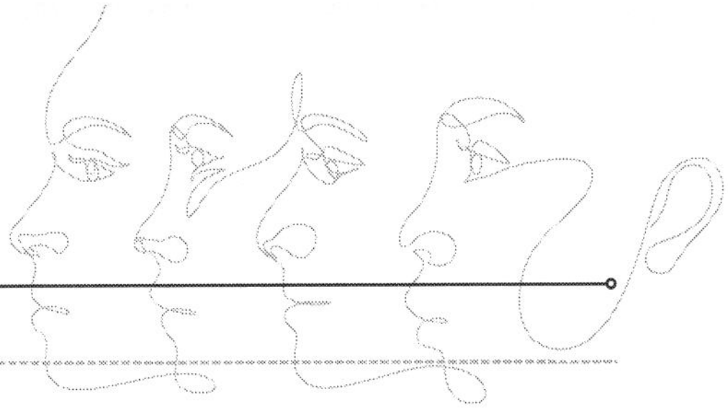

What am I excited about for next week?

Daily Planner

Date: _____

My daily
affirmations:

1 Today I am manifesting:

_____

_____

_____

2 My intentions for today are:

_____

_____

_____

3 Today I am letting go of:

_____

_____

_____

4 Today I am grateful for:

_____

_____

_____

Some of my thoughts

Daily Planner

Date: _____

1 Today I am manifesting:

_____

_____

_____

2 My intentions for today are:

_____

_____

_____

3 Today I am letting go of:

_____

_____

_____

4 Today I am grateful for:

_____

_____

_____

My daily affirmations:

Some of my thoughts

Daily Planner

Date: _____

My daily affirmations:

1 Today I am manifesting:

_____
_____
_____

2 My intentions for today are:

_____
_____
_____

3 Today I am letting go of:

_____
_____
_____

4 Today I am grateful for:

_____
_____
_____

Some of my thoughts

Daily Planner

Date: _____

1 Today I am manifesting:

_____
_____
_____

2 My intentions for today are:

_____
_____
_____

3 Today I am letting go of:

_____
_____
_____

4 Today I am grateful for:

_____
_____

My daily affirmations:

Some of my thoughts

Daily Planner

Date: _____

My daily
affirmations:

1 Today I am manifesting:

_____
_____
_____

2 My intentions for today are:

_____
_____
_____

3 Today I am letting go of:

_____
_____
_____

4 Today I am grateful for:

_____
_____

Some of my thoughts

Daily Planner

Date: _____

1 Today I am manifesting:

_____

_____

_____

2 My intentions for today are:

_____

_____

_____

3 Today I am letting go of:

_____

_____

_____

4 Today I am grateful for:

_____

_____

_____

My daily affirmations:

Some of my thoughts

Daily Planner

Date: _____

1 Today I am manifesting:

2 My intentions for today are:

3 Today I am letting go of:

4 Today I am grateful for:

My daily affirmations:

Some of my thoughts

Weekly Reflection

What was my top accomplishment this week?

What showed up that I wasn't expecting?

What made me happy this week?

What obstacles did I overcome this week?

What clues have I noticed that I am starting to manifest my dreams?

1

2

3

4

Final thoughts

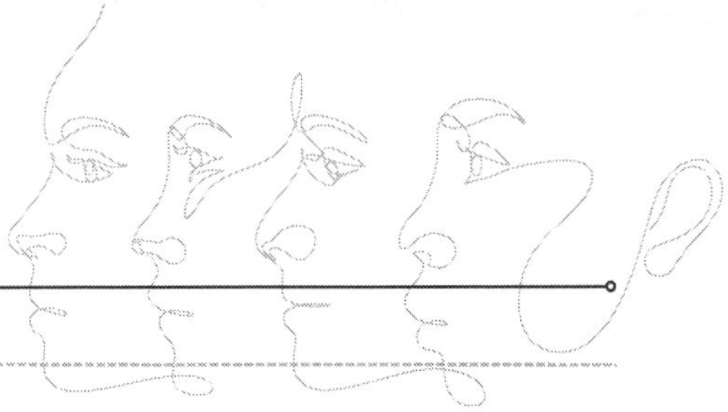

What am I excited about for next week?

Daily Planner

Date: _____

1 Today I am manifesting:

_____

_____

_____

2 My intentions for today are:

_____

_____

_____

3 Today I am letting go of:

_____

_____

_____

4 Today I am grateful for:

_____

_____

_____

Some of my thoughts

Daily Planner

Date: _____

1 Today I am manifesting:

_____

_____

_____

2 My intentions for today are:

_____

_____

_____

3 Today I am letting go of:

_____

_____

_____

4 Today I am grateful for:

_____

_____

_____

Some of my thoughts

Daily Planner

Date: _____

1 Today I am manifesting:

_____
_____
_____

2 My intentions for today are:

_____
_____
_____

3 Today I am letting go of:

_____
_____
_____

4 Today I am grateful for:

_____
_____
_____

Some of my thoughts

Daily Planner

Date: _____

1 Today I am manifesting:

_____
_____
_____

2 My intentions for today are:

_____
_____
_____

3 Today I am letting go of:

_____
_____
_____

4 Today I am grateful for:

_____
_____
_____

My daily affirmations:

Some of my thoughts

Daily Planner

Date: _____

1 Today I am manifesting:

2 My intentions for today are:

3 Today I am letting go of:

4 Today I am grateful for:

Some of my thoughts

Daily Planner

Date: _____

1 Today I am manifesting:

_____

_____

_____

2 My intentions for today are:

_____

_____

_____

3 Today I am letting go of:

_____

_____

_____

4 Today I am grateful for:

_____

_____

_____

My daily affirmations:

Some of my thoughts

Daily Planner

Date: _____

1 **Today I am manifesting:**

_____
_____
_____

2 **My intentions for today are:**

_____
_____
_____

3 **Today I am letting go of:**

_____
_____
_____

4 **Today I am grateful for:**

_____
_____
_____

My daily affirmations:

Some of my thoughts

Weekly Reflection

What was my top accomplishment this week?

_____

_____

_____

What made me happy this week?

_____

_____

What clues have I noticed that I am starting to manifest my dreams?

1 _____

2 _____

3 _____

4 _____

What showed up that I wasn't expecting?

What obstacles did I overcome this week?

Final thoughts

What am I excited about for next week?

Daily Planner

Date: _____

1 Today I am manifesting:

----

2 My intentions for today are:

----

3 Today I am letting go of:

----

4 Today I am grateful for:

My daily affirmations:

Some of my thoughts

Daily Planner

Date: _____

1 Today I am manifesting:

----

2 My intentions for today are:

----

3 Today I am letting go of:

----

4 Today I am grateful for:

Some of my thoughts

Daily Planner

Date: _____

1 **Today I am manifesting:**

_____

_____

_____

2 **My intentions for today are:**

_____

_____

3 **Today I am letting go of:**

_____

_____

_____

4 **Today I am grateful for:**

_____

_____

My daily affirmations:

Some of my thoughts

Daily Planner

Date: _____

1 Today I am manifesting:

_____

_____

_____

2 My intentions for today are:

_____

_____

_____

3 Today I am letting go of:

_____

_____

_____

4 Today I am grateful for:

_____

_____

My daily affirmations:

Some of my thoughts

Daily Planner

Date: _____

1 **Today I am manifesting:**

_____
_____
_____

2 **My intentions for today are:**

_____
_____
_____

3 **Today I am letting go of:**

_____
_____
_____

4 **Today I am grateful for:**

_____
_____

My daily affirmations.

Some of my thoughts

Daily Planner

Date: _____

① **Today I am manifesting:**

_____
_____
_____

② **My intentions for today are:**

_____
_____
_____

③ **Today I am letting go of:**

_____
_____
_____

④ **Today I am grateful for:**

_____
_____
_____

My daily affirmations:

Some of my thoughts

Daily Planner

Date: _____

1 Today I am manifesting:

_____

_____

_____

2 My intentions for today are:

_____

_____

_____

3 Today I am letting go of:

_____

_____

_____

4 Today I am grateful for:

_____

_____

Some of my thoughts

Weekly Reflection

What was my top accomplishment this week?

_____

_____

_____

What made me happy this week?

_____

_____

_____

What clues have I noticed that I am starting to manifest my dreams?

1 _____

2 _____

3 _____

4 _____

What showed up that I wasn't expecting?

What obstacles did I overcome this week?

Final thoughts

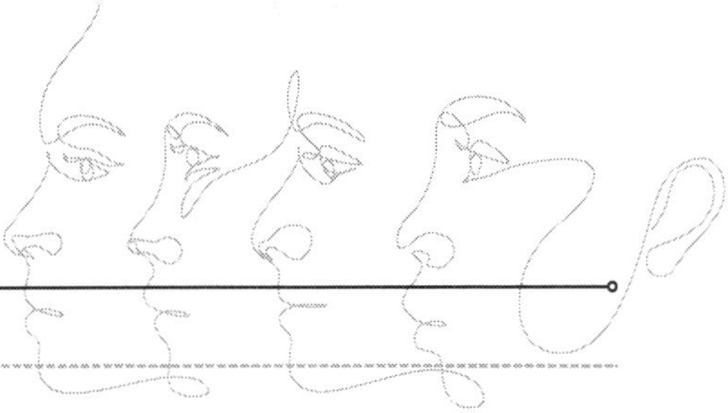

What am I excited about for next week?

Daily Planner

Date: _____

1 Today I am manifesting:

----

2 My intentions for today are:

----

3 Today I am letting go of:

----

4 Today I am grateful for:

Some of my thoughts

Daily Planner

Date: _____

1 Today I am manifesting:

_____
_____
_____

2 My intentions for today are:

_____
_____
_____

3 Today I am letting go of:

_____
_____
_____

4 Today I am grateful for:

_____
_____
_____

My daily affirmations:

Some of my thoughts

Daily Planner

Date: _____

1 Today I am manifesting:

----

2 My intentions for today are:

----

3 Today I am letting go of:

----

4 Today I am grateful for:

My daily affirmations:

Some of my thoughts

Daily Planner

Date: _____

1 Today I am manifesting:

_____

_____

_____

2 My intentions for today are:

_____

_____

_____

3 Today I am letting go of:

_____

_____

_____

4 Today I am grateful for:

_____

_____

My daily affirmations:

Some of my thoughts

Daily Planner

Date:_____

1 Today I am manifesting:

_____
_____
_____

2 My intentions for today are:

_____
_____
_____

3 Today I am letting go of:

_____
_____
_____

4 Today I am grateful for:

_____
_____

My daily affirmations:

Some of my thoughts

Daily Planner

Date: _____

1 Today I am manifesting:

_____
_____
_____

2 My intentions for today are:

_____
_____
_____

3 Today I am letting go of:

_____
_____
_____

4 Today I am grateful for:

_____
_____

Some of my thoughts

Daily Planner

Date: _____

1 Today I am manifesting:

_____

_____

_____

2 My intentions for today are:

_____

_____

_____

3 Today I am letting go of:

_____

_____

_____

4 Today I am grateful for:

_____

_____

_____

Some of my thoughts

Weekly Reflection

What was my top accomplishment this week?

_____

_____

_____

What made me happy this week?

_____

_____

_____

What clues have I noticed that I am starting to manifest my dreams?

1 _____

2 _____

3 _____

4 _____

What showed up that I wasn't expecting?

What obstacles did I overcome this week?

Final thoughts

What am I excited about for next week?

Daily Planner

Date: _____

1 Today I am manifesting:

2 My intentions for today are:

3 Today I am letting go of:

4 Today I am grateful for:

My daily affirmations:

Some of my thoughts

Daily Planner

Date: _____

My daily affirmations:

1 Today I am manifesting:

_____

_____

_____

2 My intentions for today are:

_____

_____

_____

3 Today I am letting go of:

_____

_____

_____

4 Today I am grateful for:

_____

_____

Some of my thoughts

Daily Planner

Date: _____

1 Today I am manifesting:

_____
_____
_____

2 My intentions for today are:

_____
_____
_____

3 Today I am letting go of:

_____
_____

4 Today I am grateful for:

_____
_____

My daily affirmations:

Daily Planner

Date: _____

1   Today I am manifesting:

----

2   My intentions for today are:

----

3   Today I am letting go of:

----

4   Today I am grateful for:

My daily affirmations:

Some of my thoughts

Daily Planner

Date: _____

1 Today I am manifesting:

_____
_____
_____

2 My intentions for today are:

_____
_____
_____

3 Today I am letting go of:

_____
_____
_____

4 Today I am grateful for:

_____
_____
_____

My daily affirmations:

Some of my thoughts

Daily Planner

Date: _____

1 Today I am manifesting:

_____

_____

_____

2 My intentions for today are:

_____

_____

_____

3 Today I am letting go of:

_____

_____

_____

4 Today I am grateful for:

_____

_____

_____

Some of my thoughts

Daily Planner

Date: _____

1 **Today I am manifesting:**

_____
_____
_____

2 **My intentions for today are:**

_____
_____
_____

3 **Today I am letting go of:**

_____
_____
_____

4 **Today I am grateful for:**

_____
_____
_____

My daily affirmations:

Some of my thoughts

Weekly Reflection

What was my top accomplishment this week?

_____

_____

_____

What made me happy this week?

_____

_____

What clues have I noticed that I am starting to manifest my dreams?

1 _____

2 _____

3 _____

4 _____

What showed up that I wasn't expecting?

What obstacles did I overcome this week?

Final thoughts

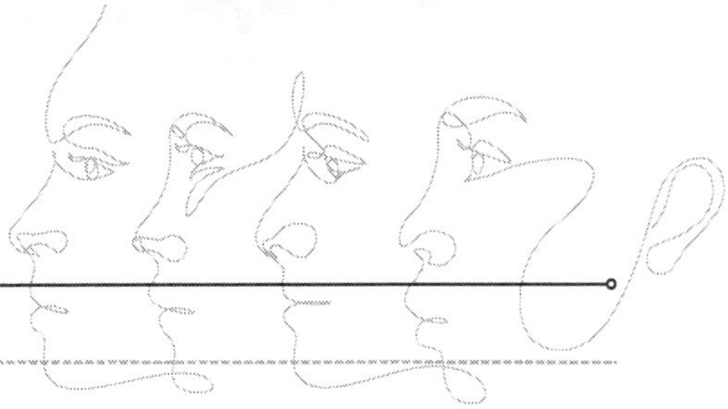

What am I excited about for next week?

Daily Planner

Date: _____

My daily affirmations:

1 Today I am manifesting:

----

2 My intentions for today are:

----

3 Today I am letting go of:

----

4 Today I am grateful for:

Some of my thoughts

Daily Planner

Date: _____

My daily affirmations:

1 Today I am manifesting:

....

....

....

2 My intentions for today are:

....

....

....

3 Today I am letting go of:

....

....

....

4 Today I am grateful for:

....

....

....

Some of my thoughts

Daily Planner

Date: _____

My daily affirmations:

1 Today I am manifesting:

_____

_____

_____

2 My intentions for today are:

_____

_____

_____

3 Today I am letting go of:

_____

_____

_____

4 Today I am grateful for:

_____

_____

Some of my thoughts

Daily Planner

Date: _____

1 Today I am manifesting:

_____
_____
_____

2 My intentions for today are:

_____
_____
_____

3 Today I am letting go of:

_____
_____
_____

4 Today I am grateful for:

_____
_____
_____

My daily affirmations:

Some of my thoughts

Daily Planner

Date: _____

My daily affirmations:

1 Today I am manifesting:

_____

_____

_____

2 My intentions for today are:

_____

_____

_____

3 Today I am letting go of:

_____

_____

_____

4 Today I am grateful for:

_____

_____

Some of my thoughts

Daily Planner

Date: _____

1 Today I am manifesting:

_____
_____
_____

2 My intentions for today are:

_____
_____
_____

3 Today I am letting go of:

_____
_____
_____

4 Today I am grateful for:

_____
_____

My daily affirmations:

Daily Planner

Date: _____

1 **Today I am manifesting:**

_____
_____
_____

2 **My intentions for today are:**

_____
_____
_____

3 **Today I am letting go of:**

_____
_____
_____

4 **Today I am grateful for:**

_____
_____
_____

My daily affirmations:

Some of my thoughts

Weekly Reflection

What was my top accomplishment this week?

_____

_____

_____

What showed up that I wasn't expecting?

What made me happy this week?

_____

_____

_____

What obstacles did I overcome this week?

What clues have I noticed that I am starting to manifest my dreams?

1

2

3

4

Final thoughts

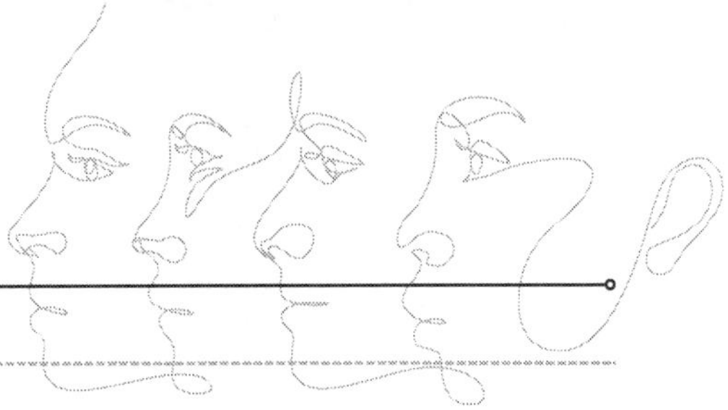

What am I excited about for next week?

Daily Planner

Date: _____

My daily affirmations:

1 Today I am manifesting:

_____
_____
_____

2 My intentions for today are:

_____
_____
_____

3 Today I am letting go of:

_____
_____
_____

4 Today I am grateful for:

_____
_____
_____

Some of my thoughts

Daily Planner

Date: _____

1 Today I am manifesting:

_____

_____

_____

2 My intentions for today are:

_____

_____

_____

3 Today I am letting go of:

_____

_____

_____

4 Today I am grateful for:

_____

_____

_____

My daily affirmations:

Some of my thoughts

Daily Planner

Date: _____

My daily affirmations:

1 Today I am manifesting:

_____
_____
_____

2 My intentions for today are:

_____
_____
_____

3 Today I am letting go of:

_____
_____
_____

4 Today I am grateful for:

_____
_____

Some of my thoughts

Daily Planner

Date: _____

1 Today I am manifesting:

_____

_____

_____

2 My intentions for today are:

_____

_____

_____

3 Today I am letting go of:

_____

_____

_____

4 Today I am grateful for:

_____

_____

My daily affirmations:

Some of my thoughts

Daily Planner

Date: _____

1 Today I am manifesting:

_____
_____
_____

2 My intentions for today are:

_____
_____
_____

3 Today I am letting go of:

_____
_____
_____

4 Today I am grateful for:

_____
_____
_____

My daily affirmations:

Some of my thoughts

Daily Planner

Date: _____

1   Today I am manifesting:

_____

_____

_____

2   My intentions for today are:

_____

_____

_____

3   Today I am letting go of:

_____

_____

_____

4   Today I am grateful for:

_____

_____

_____

My daily affirmations:

Some of my thoughts

Daily Planner

Date: _____

1 Today I am manifesting:

_____

_____

_____

2 My intentions for today are:

_____

_____

_____

3 Today I am letting go of:

_____

_____

_____

4 Today I am grateful for:

_____

_____

My daily affirmations:

Some of my thoughts

Weekly Reflection

What was my top accomplishment this week?

What made me happy this week?

What clues have I noticed that I am starting to manifest my dreams?

1

2

3

4

What showed up that I wasn't expecting?

What obstacles did I overcome this week?

Final thoughts

What am I excited about for next week?

Some of my thoughts

Some of my thoughts

Some of my thoughts

Some of my thoughts

Some of my thoughts

Thank you for purchasing this journal.

If you have found value in this material please consider leaving feedback so that others may benefit as well.

Your support means so much!

Thank you,

Sophia L. Joyce

Just scan this code to leave feedback on Amazon

★★★★★

Or use the link below:
https://amzn.to/3fArj4p

Find my author page and more books here:

Made in the USA
Columbia, SC
29 December 2024

50847951R00083